Old GOVAN

by

Bill Spalding

First Published in the United Kingdom, 1994
By Richard Stenlake, Ochiltree Sawmill, The Lade, Ochiltree, Ayrshire KA18 2NX
Telephone: 01290 700266

ISBN 1-872074-47-2

Summertown Road

GOVAN.

The burgh mottto was *Nothing Without Labour*

INTRODUCTION

There have been communities living on the site of Govan for many hundreds of years and St Constantine chose this spot, situated on the south bank of the Clyde, for the foundation of a monastery in the sixth century. Exploiting the natural resources of the river, Govan grew steadily from then on, and by the beginning of the nineteenth century was a village of about 2,500 people. Most of its population were weavers and salmon fishers.

Hampered by the shallowness of the Clyde, which made navigation up the river impossible for large vessels, the authorities in Glasgow started to deepen the river from around 1770. This, and in particular the construction of Glasgow harbour at the Broomielaw, meant that the shipyards established there were forced to relocate. Napier's yard moved to Govan, and in due course many other yards were set up alongside it. As a result of this industrial activity, Govan mushroomed.

The shipyards required thousands of workers to staff them, and a steady influx of people from the West Highlands and Ireland arrived in Govan. In order to raise the money to provide the developing village with the amenities of a small town, Govan became a burgh in 1864. Soon row upon row of tenements were constructed to provide accommodation for the new workforce, and the town's population had risen to over 90,000 by 1912.

Changing economic conditions after World War Two led to a dramatic decline in the shipbuilding industry. Many of the yards were forced to close through lack of orders, and today only one remains operative - the yard that was formerly Fairfield's. However, even during the industry's heyday, work at the yards was not always steady. The following extract is taken from the message on the postcard pictured on page 48, postmarked 1904:

"Tuesday the 20th was the latest date appointed by the Admiralty for the receipt of tenders for the two new battleships from Clyde, Barrow and Tyne firms, so I suppose it will not be long now ere we know what to expect here. Nothing else is offering at present, and William thinks it will be the fate of the firm one way or the other now. Great distress is feared this winter."

Govan life was not solely identified with shipbuilding, and other important local employers included the Scottish Cooperative Wholesale Society, which established an enormous productive works at Shieldhall in the late nineteenth century. However, the influence of the shipbuilding industry is a profound one that is still felt today. The large number of local landmarks which are the legacy of the yard owners, and the yards and docks themselves, all serve as visible reminders of the burgh's shipbuilding heritage.

The Pond Elder Park. Govan.

Elder Park was presented to the Burgh of Govan in 1885 by Mrs Elder in memory of her late husband, who had owned the shipbuilding yard that eventually became Fairfield's. Opening day was declared a public holiday and a parade marched from Paisley Road Toll to the park gates through streets decorated with flags and bunting. The Elder Park Model Yacht Club, founded two years later, used the newly created pond for its club events, including an open regattta and regular matches against other Glasgow clubs.

In 1890 an area at the western end of the park was set aside to house a deer which had been brought to Scotland from Japan. Two fallow deer from Arran were added and later, in 1896, a guanaco (a type of llama), which came from Patagonia.

The Band Stand, Elder Park, Govan.

RELIABLE SERIES.

WITH XMAS GREETINGS AND ALL GOOD WI

Now gone, the bandstand at Elder Park was a focal point for the local community. As well as army bands (both regular and territorial), there were a number of local burgh and works bands who played there. Govan also played host to visiting outfits which travelled from places such as Airdrie and Kilsyth.

The Govan Police Band in full formal regalia.

Govan Citadel Band, 1915. The Salvation Army came to Scotland in 1879 and in the early days was greeted with jeers and mud- and stone-throwing. However, public relations gradually improved and the Govan Citadel Band was regarded with great respect. It was considered to be one of the foremost bands in the army.

Mrs Rachel Green outside her shop at 18-20 Plantation Street, 1925.

Elder Library, Govan.

In addition to donating a park to the burgh, John Elder's widow also provided local library and hospital facilities. The Elder Library, above, was opened in September 1903 by Andrew Carnegie.

Even today, the Elder name is prominent in Govan and the surrounding area. In addition to the park and library, there is an Elder Cottage Hospital, and the Elder Memorial Chapel in Partick's Western Infirmary.

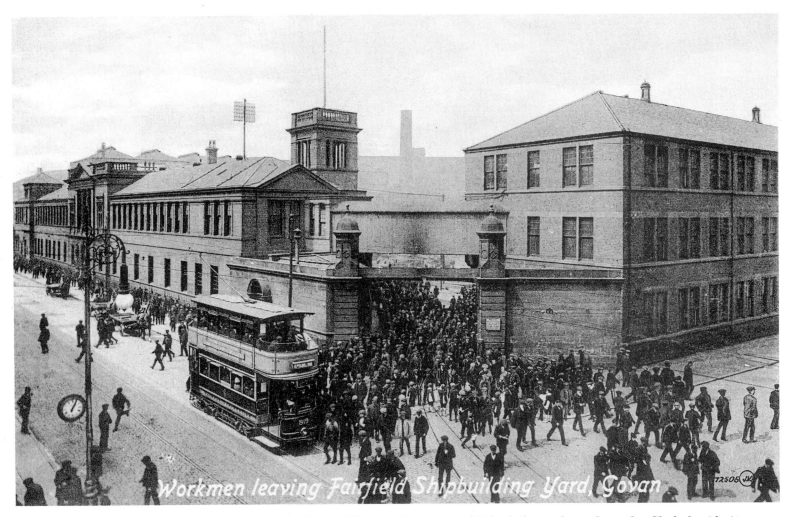

Workmen leaving Fairfield Shipbuilding Yard, Govan

Govan owed much of its prosperity to the shipbuilding yards that established themselves along the Clyde beside it, and companies such as Fairfield's were major employers in the burgh. Founded in 1834 by Randolph and Cunliffe, the Fairfield Yard has changed ownership several times. It still operates today - as Kvaerner Govan Ltd - although the workforce is a fraction of its former number.

The number and size of the ships in this picture of the Fairfield Dock provides a sharp contrast with the relative inactivity of recent years.

Fairfield Shipbuilding Yard, Govan.

Showing largest crane in the world, height of crane 170 feet, length of jib 258 feet, lifting capacity 250 tons.

"Just a view of the yard. The Empress of Canada was completed over two years ago - this is an old picture(!) X marks where I'm working - the engine shop" (postmarked 1924)

Using the tramlines, the Fairfield train ran along Govan Road to the yard, carrying workers from the railway sidings of the Glasgow and Paisley Joint Railway at Govan Cross. Here the train is passing the foot of Helen Street.

An atmospheric view, circa 1912, of a cross-river ferry approaching Partick, with Stephen's Linthouse yard in the background.

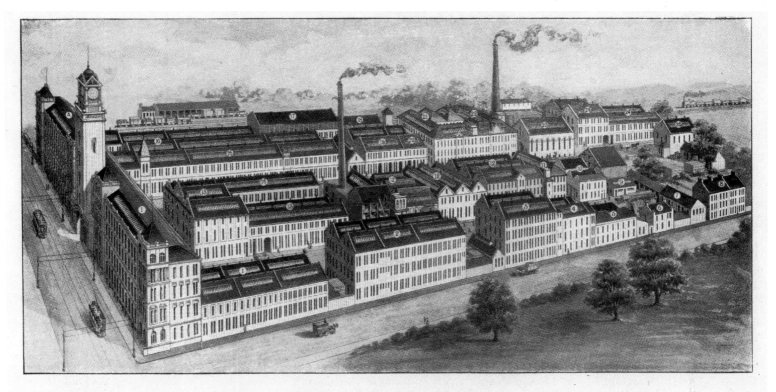

Productive Works, Shieldhall, Govan.

(A) Portion of Front Building not yet allocated.

1. Printing Department.
2. Cabinet Factory.
3. Hosiery Factory.
4. Coffee Essence.
5. Brush Factory.

6. Firemaster's House.
7. Joiner's Workshop.
8. Workmen's Dwellings.
9. Cooperage.
10. Mechanical, Elect'l.

11. Tinware.
12. Preserve Works.
13. Tailoring Factory.
14. Artisan Clothing.
15. Dining Rooms, etc.

16. Boot Factory.
17. Currying Works.
18. Tannery.
19. Confectionery Works.
20. Pickle Works.

21-22. Chemical Dept.
23. Power Station.
24. Tobacco Factory.
25. Stables.

In addition to the local shipbuilding yards, the Scottish Cooperative Wholesale Society's works at Shieldhall also employed many local people. Founded in 1868, the SCWS initially established itself as a wholesaler supplying smaller retail societies. However, because manufacturers proved so unreliable, the society began to undertake production work for itself. As this enterprise expanded, new premises were required.

Cabinet Factory, Shieldhall.

CABINET FACTORY ESTABLISHED 1884.

SCWS production began with the acquisition of a tailoring business in 1881. A cabinet factory and boot and shoe manufacturing works followed, and at this stage the Shieldhall site was acquired.

Shieldhall, Govan.

In addition to the works in Govan, the SCWS was active all over Scotland. Flour milling took place in Edinburgh and Leith, and the Regent Mills on the Kelvin at Partick Bridge produced "Lofty Peak" flour. The Ettrick Tweed Mill (Selkirk) and Falkirk Linen Factory were subsequently acquired to provide cloth for the Shieldhall clothing factories.

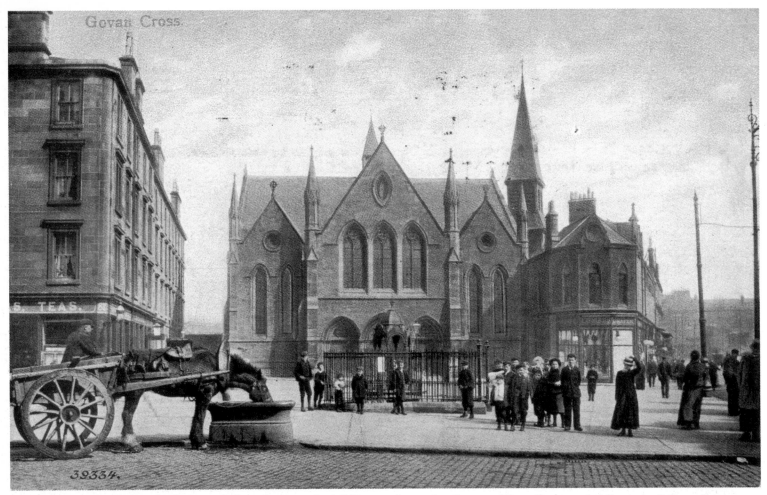

At one time Govan had several churches serving different denominations , although many of these buildings have now been demolished. The Church of St Mary's at Govan Cross (pictured above) was built in 1873 to accomodate a congregation formed as part of Dr Robert Buchanan's Church Extension Movement. Before the building was constructed services were held in Govan Town Hall in Robert Street. St Mary's has since united with two other congregations, most recently in 1982, and is now known as the New Govan Church.

OLD GOVAN PARISH CHURCH

Left: The site of Old Govan Parish Church is a historic one. In the middle of the sixth century, St Constantine founded a monastery on or near the site, and there have been churches dedicated to him there ever since. In the 1880's it was proposed to replace the church pictured with a new one. Old Govan Parish Church was dismantled brick by brick, and rebuilt in Golspie Street as Elderpark Church.

Right: The building which replaced Old Govan Parish Church was dedicated in 1888 and is still standing today. Govan Parish was not confined to the south of the Clyde, where it stretched from Polmadie in the east to Renfrew in the west, but also took in areas on the north bank of the river. People living in Partick, who were in the Established Church of Scotland, had to take a ferry over the Clyde in order to worship. The picture shows a Salvation Army service being conducted outside the church.

Published by M'Gregor & Co.

Hill's Trust Public School, Govan

The Band begins on Saturday.

Do you recognise the buildin... We have had the Inspectors y... times since December. A.M...

Hill's Trust School was the legacy of Abraham Hill, who had been born in Govan and became a successful merchant in Wolverhampton. In 1757 he bequeathed a trust fund to buy land in the Govan area. The income from this land was to be paid to the Govan schoolmaster to educate children from the poorest local families. Somewhat undemocratically, preference was to be given to pupils named Hill! The correspondent on this card says "we have had the inspectors seven times since December" (the card was posted in May), and also observes that the building "looks better outside than in!"

High School, Govan.

The Govan High School was built in Langlands Road in 1910 and survived until the 1970's when it was gutted by fire. A new health clinic was built on the site and a replacement school erected in Ardnish Street, off Shieldhall Road.

The manuscript caption on the back of this photograph of the Windsor Street Laundry is self-explanatory: "This is some of the shirt ironers and also the post that brings us the letters. Puzzle - find me. From Mary."

Govan Road circa 1925. The boy bent over in the middle of the street has probably just placed a penny on the tram line for it to be flattened by the next passing tram.

Just visible at the right of this picture of Govan Cross is the Aitken Memorial Fountain (obscured by the decorative canopy). John Aitken had a particular interest in the poor of Govan and played an important role in the area as a doctor. By the age of 21 he was a "Licentiate of the Faculty of Physicians and Surgeons" and immediately set up practice in Govan. He subsequently became the local police surgeon and Burgh Medical Officer, and also provided medical services for the collieries at Ibrox and Drumoyne.

Pearce Statue and Lyceum Theatre, Govan

Individuals such as William Pearce and John Elder played important roles in bringing prosperity to Govan. Although much of the work provided by the industries that they controlled was undoubtedly unpleasant and underpaid, the local community understood the importance of such businessmen to the burgh. In this seemingly posed shot of town life, policemen and passers-by are gathered around the Pearce statue, erected by the populace in 1894.

Govan Cross.

Govan Cross was the hub of the Burgh with Water Row (to the right) leading to the ferry, and the subway, which opened in 1896, to the left of shot. The building visible in the distance with the clock on it is the Pearce Institute. William Pearce became the sole owner of the Fairfield's yard after the death of John Elder, and like his predecessor invested some of his fortune in philanthropic concerns. The institute was erected in the early 1900's as a community centre providing a range of different facilities. These included men's and women's reading rooms and clubs, a library, a gymnasium, 'retiring rooms', and cooking and laundry departments. The Pearce Institute remains an active community centre today.

28

A better view of the Pearce Institute, with a white-clad traffic policeman in the foreground, recalling the days before traffic lights were universal!

Lyceum Theatre, Govan

The Lyceum Music Hall opened in style in 1899 with a performance of Carmen by the Carl Rosa Opera Company. The growing popularity of 'cinematographic entertainments' meant that many theatres were converted into cinemas and the Lyceum became a full time picture-house by 1923. After the building was burnt down in the thirties, a new cinema, built in typical art deco style, was opened seating two thousand people. The building is now devoted to bingo-playing.

LANGLANDS ROAD AT CROSSLOAN ROAD, GOVAN, GLASGOW

At the peak of cinema fever, Govan had the choice of four venues: the Elder, Lyceum, Plaza and Vogue. In addition to these, three more cinemas were on the Burgh's boundaries, while the subway meant that another half-dozen picture-houses were within easy reach in Partick. The Vogue Cinema was situated where Langlands Road and Crossloan Road met. Its owner, George Singleton, ran an empire of seven cinemas, including the Vogue. This fine building has now been demolished and flats occupy the site.

Govan Road. The building on the left, which was originally Fairfield's yard, still stands today although it now operates as Kvaerner Govan Ltd.

Govan Road, Govan.

This view, taken further down Govan Road than the one opposite, looks east from Fairfield's yard. The crowd of work-men outside the yard are waiting to return to work after the dinner break. The boys in the middle of the street have bare feet, and testify to the poverty-stricken times. On the right, the pub with the clock outside it is at the corner of Elder Street.

Govan Road at the corner of Reid Street.

Looking east along Govan Road, the first street on the right is Broomloan Road. On its corner, the building with the arched windows is a branch of the Glasgow Savings Bank. More barefoot boys!

Govan Docks.

The site of the graving docks in Govan was initially home to the burgh's first Free Church. When the church moved to new premises in Summertown Road the old building was converted into a theatre. Afterwards it became a third-rate music hall, and later a lodging house for Russian soldiers who were sent to man the Peter the Great. Three graving or dry docks were then constructed on the site, and were used to carry out work on those parts of ships that were usually submerged.

The nearest dock contains two ships. In the foreground is the Waverley paddle-steamer, sunk at Dunkirk in 1940. In this picture the steps on the side of the docks, which allowed workmen access to the hull of the ship, can be seen. Due to an unfortunate camera angle the ship in the other dock appears to have an extra funnel built onto its bows!

Princes Dock (originally to be called Cessnock Dock) was built on the lands of Cessnock on a site which had previously been used as a market garden. Work began in 1890, and Govan Road had to be realigned to accomodate the development. It was formally opened in 1897 by the Duchess of York. The dock was used to export coal from the Lanarkshire pits and to import iron ore and limestone from elsewhere.

Princes Dock, Govan. *We skiy the other side of the river from this. E. W. W. 10/8/04*

This 130-ton crane points to the three inner basins of Princes dock. It was used to load locomotives from the North British loco works in Polmadie onto ships which then transported them all over the world. In July 1971 the main quays were closed down, sheds flattened, cranes removed, and the basins (except for the canting basin) infilled with rubble from demolished tenements, and the St Enoch Station and Hotel. The site was redeveloped by the Scottish Development Agency for the Glasgow Garden Festival in 1988.

Govan Road, Linthouse

The street on the left of the picture is Holmfauld Road, leading to the ferry from Linthouse to Whiteinch. The horse and cart has just passed a branch of Cochrane's, a chain of grocery stores that were once widespread and popular. An old-fashioned police box, with its lamp on top, is just visible outside Cochrane's.

Linthouse, Govan

This view shows Burghhead Drive with a restaurant on the corner and next to it a barber's shop with the once-familiar red and white striped pole outside. Beyond that is Holmfauldhead Drive.

Linthouse, Glasgow

Soon after the turn of the century, Govan developed a comprehensive network of electric trams, powered by overhead cables. These replaced the earlier horse-drawn omnibuses.

John Irwin's store was in Govan Road at the corner of Helen Street, and later became a branch of the Glasgow South Cooperative Society. As was quite common, there is a dental surgery above the local shop. There are advertising boards posted on each street corner - a common sight in the days before a dentist had to be qualified. Advertising by dentists was banned for a long time and has only been reintroduced recently.

Not strictly in Govan, I know, but the publisher insisted I include this 1915 photo of Paisley Road East at Kingston, now lost under the piers of the famous road bridge.

Nearby was the depot of Wordie and Co, a firm of carrriers with branches all over Scotland. The steam lorry seen here would have been a familiar sight in Govan around 1912.

In addition to cross-Clyde ferry services, 'up and down' ferries operated along the river under the management of the Clyde Navigation Trust. They began in 1884 with four small steamers, of a type known as Cluthas, and became so popular that by 1896 twelve passenger vessels were sailing between Stockwell Bridge and Whiteinch. The ten stopping places on the route included Govan (Highland Lane) and Linthouse. The vessels were called 'penny steamers' because of the fare they charged, which undercut that of the horse-drawn trams. However, they were hit badly by the advent of the electric trams, and the last run was on 30 November 1903. The small vessel on the left of this picture is a Clutha.

Donaldson Liner T. S. S. "Athenia".

Ships that berthed at Govan also travelled international routes. Vessels belonging to the Donaldson Line sailed to America and eventually dominated the Scotland-Canada run. This postcard is one of the many brought out in the earlier 1900's depicting the 'Hands Across The Sea' motif, issued when emigration to Canada and the United States was at its height. The Athenia was sunk by a German submarine, with the loss of 112 lives, only a few hours after war was declared on Sunday 3 September 1939.

It was important for the people of Govan to be able to cross the Clyde as there were shipyards on both sides of the river, and some residents of the town worked in the mills in Partick. This picture shows the ferry pay booth on the Govan side of the Clyde, with the attendant who manned its cast iron turnstile. The torn poster on the right has a table of rates for ferry crossings.

When passengers disembarked from the ferry at Govan in the 1800's, they made their way up to Govan Cross via Water Row, at that time lined on the west side with whitewashed cottages. Around here was the Ferrie-Bot inn. John McNaire, assisted by his wife, Janet Dunlop, kept it and also owned the ferry. After the sermon at Govan Parish Church on Sundays, the kirk bell was rung to warn the ferryman to prepare his boat, so that Partick passengers could be ferried back home.

Govan Ferry

The earliest ferries were ordinary rowing boats, but as the size and volume of traffic crossing the Clyde increased, mechanically powered vessels were required. This steam ferry dragged itself across the river via two submerged chains connnected to sprocket wheels on board which were turned by the ferry's engines.

WTI.3.

This more advanced ferry used a deck that could be raised or lowered through a range of fourteen feet so as to be at the same level as the quay at any state of the tide. It was introduced in 1890 and crossed from Barclay Curle's shipyard at Whiteinch to Stephen's Shipyard at Linthouse.

H.M.S. Indomitable.

LAUNCHED 16TH MARCH 1907,
FAIRFIELD SHIPYARD, GOVAN.

Particulars.

Length—530ft.
Breadth—78ft. 6in.
Draught—26ft.
Weight of hull—9660 tons.
Displacement—17,250 tons.
H.P.—41,000.
Speed—25 knots.
Coal capacity at load draught—1000 tons.
Cost—£1,730,000.

The construction of a large ship such as the Indomitable was a colossal undertaking, requiring tens of thousands of man-hours to complete it. Postcards such as this were produced to celebrate the launch of these ships and to provide a souvenir of the event.